D1573300

DISCARDED

North American Historical Atlases

TEXAS

AND THE

FAR WEST

North American
Historical Atlases

TEXAS

AND THE

FAR WEST

Rebecca Stefoff

BENCHMARK BOOKS

MARSHALL CAVENDISH
NEW YORK

Benchmark Books
Marshall Cavendish Corporation
99 White Plains Road
Tarrytown, New York 10591

• • •

Library of Congress Cataloging-in-Publication Data
Stefoff, Rebecca, 1951-
Texas and the Far West/by Rebecca Stefoff
p. cm—(North American historical atlases)
Includes bibliographical references and index.
Summary: Details the American expansion into Texas and the far west from the late eighteenth-to the
mid-nineteenth century, including information on the Oregon Trail, the war with Mexico, and the California gold rush.
ISBN 0-7614-1345-6 (lib.bdg.)
1. West (U.S.)—History—Juvenile literature.   2. West (U.S.)—History—Maps—Juvenile literature.
3. United States—Territorial expansion—Juvenile literature.   4. United States—Territorial expansion—Maps—
Juvenile literature.   5. Frontier and pioneer life—West (U.S.)—Juvenile literature.   6. Frontier and pioneer life—
West (U.S.)—Maps—Juvenile literature.   7. Southwest, New—History—Juvenile literature.   8. Southwest, New—History—
Maps—Juvenile literature.   [1. West (U.S.)—History.   2. United States—Territorial expansion.
3. Frontier and pioneer life—West (U.S.)   4. Southwest, New—History.]   I. Title.
F591 .S8225   2002   2001043817   978—dc21

• • •

Printed in Hong Kong
1 3 5 7 8 6 4 2

• • •

Book Designer: Judith Turziano
Photo Researcher: Candlepants Incorporated

• • •

CREDITS
Front Cover: Map of Mexico, California and Texas by J. Rapkin 1851, reproduced with
permission from the collection of the Library of Congress, Washington, D.C.
Back Cover: Smithsonian American Art Museum, Washington, D.C.

The photographs in this book are used by permission and through the courtesy of: *Corbis:* 20, 32; Christie's Images: 2–3; Francis G. Mayer: 7;
Geoffrey Clements: 9; Michael Nicholson: 8; Bettmann: 13, 19, 23, 24, 27, 28, 31, 35, 36, 37, 41; *Art Resource, NY:* National Museum of American Art,
Washington, D.C.: 12; Smithsonian American Art Museum, Washington, D.C.: 17; *Colorado Historical Society:* 14.

Contents

Chapter One

BEYOND
THE ROCKY
MOUNTAINS

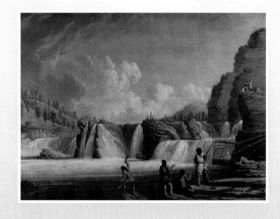

In 1783, the Treaty of Paris ended the American Revolution and established the United States as an independent country with its western border at the Mississippi River. Just twenty years later, in 1803, the United States doubled its size by buying the Louisiana Territory from France. Everything between the Atlantic Coast and the Rocky Mountains now belonged to the United States, except for Florida and Texas, which were claimed by Spain. Americans lost no time exploring their new territory—and the lands beyond its western boundary.

Explorers of the Pacific Coast

People had been exploring North America's Pacific coastline for centuries. In the 1520s, the Spanish founded a colony in Mexico and began sailing north along the coast, fighting the southward-blowing winds. In 1542, Juan Rodríguez Cabrillo took three ships north and discovered San Diego Bay. Cabrillo died on the trip, but some of his men continued as far north as Oregon. The English were also interested in the Pacific. In 1579, adventurer Sir Francis Drake claimed to have landed briefly on the California coast while sailing around the world. Twenty-three years later, Sebastián Vizcaíno discovered how dramatic northern California's weather can be. Just short of San Francisco Bay, he turned his ships back to Mexico because of "cold so great they thought they would be frozen," a historian of his day wrote.

England's Sir Francis Drake claimed to have landed on the California coast in 1579. Although many modern historians do not take the claim seriously, for centuries, California appeared as Nova Albion (Latin for "New England") on English maps.

By the late eighteenth century, European explorers had mapped most of the Pacific shoreline. In 1775, Spanish captain Bruno de Hezeta glimpsed the mouth of a mighty river on the Oregon coast. During the 1790s, two

British captains, James Cook and George Vancouver, also tried to find this river, but were thwarted by stormy weather.

Americans Reach the Far West

An American sea captain had better luck. Robert Gray of Boston had already sailed to Oregon in 1787, making him the first American to reach the Pacific Coast. In 1792 Gray returned to Oregon and found the river Hezeta had spotted. Today that river bears the name of Gray's ship, the *Columbia*. Hearing of Gray's success, Vancouver came back at once and sailed up the river.

Another explorer arrived by land. Alexander Mackenzie was a British fur trader looking for a water route from British Canada to the Pacific. The first river he followed led him north through Canada to the Arctic Ocean instead. He named it the River of Disappointment, but today we call it the Mackenzie in his honor. Mackenzie didn't give up his quest. In 1792 to

American artist George Caleb Bingham painted **Fur Traders Descending the Missouri** *around 1845 afteer traveling on the Mississppi rivers. The painting celebrates the voyages of the fur-seeking men who became leading explorers of the West.*

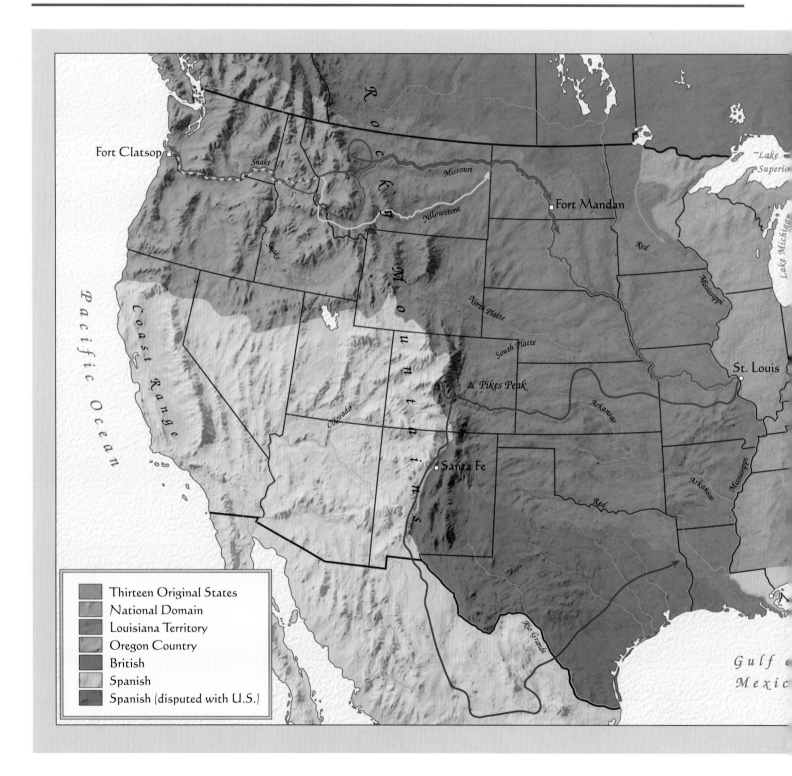

Fort Clatsop

Snake

Missouri

Yellowstone

Fort Mandan

Snake

Red

Mississippi

North Platte

South Platte

Pikes Peak

St. Louis

Arkansas

Colorado

Santa Fe

Arkansas

Mississippi

Red

Rio Grande

Pacific Ocean

Coast Range

R o c k y

M o u n t a i n s

Lake Superior

Lake Michigan

Gulf of Mexico

Thirteen Original States
National Domain
Louisiana Territory
Oregon Country
British
Spanish
Spanish (disputed with U.S.)

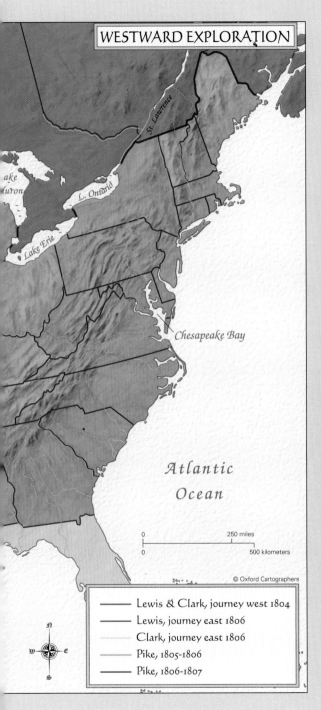

St. Lawrence

L. Ontario

Lake Erie

Chesapeake Bay

Atlantic
Ocean

0   250 miles

0   500 kilometers

© Oxford Cartographers

——— Lewis & Clark, journey west 1804
——— Lewis, journey east 1806
——— Clark, journey east 1806
——— Pike, 1805-1806
——— Pike, 1806-1807

One of history's most spectacular real-estate deals took place in 1803, when President Thomas Jefferson bought the Louisiana Territory from France. The Louisiana Purchase (shown here in brown) doubled the size of the United States overnight. It also gave Americans control of the Mississippi River, a vital shipping route. The ink was barely dry on the paperwork of the Louisiana Purchase when Jefferson, who had long been curious about the western lands, sent army officers Meriwether Lewis and William Clark on a mission of exploration—not just to the Rocky Mountains, the far border of the new American territory, but beyond them, all the way to the Pacific. Farther south, Zebulon Pike ventured into Spanish territory beyond the Louisiana Purchase on a mission that was part exploration, part espionage.

1793 he traveled from eastern Canada across the Rockies to the Pacific. He was the first white person to cross the continent north of Mexico.

News of Mackenzie's journey made Americans curious about the Pacific Northwest—and fearful that Britain would claim it. As soon as President Thomas Jefferson had bought the Louisiana Territory in 1803, he sent army officers Meriwether Lewis and William Clark west from St. Louis on a mission of exploration. They reached the Pacific Coast and returned triumphantly to St. Louis in 1806. Lewis and Clark proved that Americans could travel overland to the Pacific Northwest, although the trip was long, and in places, difficult. Another army offi-cer, Zebulon Pike, explored Minnesota and then traveled through Spanish territory in the Southwest. Americans' curiosity about the area beyond the Mississippi was growing. It was only a matter of time before that little-known land would be thoroughly explored.

Mountain Men

The fur trade was responsible for the first permanent American settlement on the Pacific. The warm, waterproof furs of sea otters and beavers were very valuable in the early nineteenth century, and adventurers sought them in the new western lands. In 1811, an East Coast businessman named John Jacob Astor

At the yearly meeting called the **rendezvous,** *fur trappers and Indians barter goods in this painting by twentieth-century American artist Elizabeth Lochrie. These gatherings were big business. At the 1826 rendezvous in Ogden, Utah, one St. Louis merchant showed up with one hundred pack animals to carry the beaver pelts he planned to buy.*

sent men by land and sea to establish a trading post at the mouth of the Columbia River, where they could get furs from the local Native Americans. The traders' fort later became Astoria, Oregon.

The fur trade also drew men to the Rocky Mountains and the Great Basin, the region west of the Rockies. Explorers reported that the western streams and lakes teemed with beaver, and soon traders and trappers were working their way west. During the 1820s, a band of these hardy people—known as mountain men—lived and worked in the wilderness. They trapped animals and traded goods such as guns, knives, and cloth to the Indians for furs. Each year they met somewhere in the Rocky Mountains to sell their furs to merchants from St. Louis or the East Coast. They called this gathering the *rendezvous,* which is French for "meeting," because some of the early trappers were French Canadian. The rendezvous was a time of "mirth, songs, dancing, shouting, trading, running, jumping, singing, racing, target-shooting, yarns, frolic, with all sorts of extravagances that white men or Indians could invent," one mountain man later recalled.

Many of the mountain men lived among Native Americans, and some married Indian women. They spent much time scouting unknown territory looking for new sources of fur, and they discovered marvels such as the geysers of Yellowstone and the Great Salt Lake.

Historians think that mountain man Jim Bridger was the first white person to see Utah's Great Salt Lake. Bridger described tasting the lake's water, which was so salty that he thought he had reached an arm of the Pacific Ocean.

Some knew more about the geography of western North America than any explorer or mapmaker. The greatest traveler among them was Jedediah Smith, the first white person to cross

A BLACK AMERICAN IN THE WEST

 James P. Beckwourth of Virginia was a famous mountain man whose ancestors were both black and white. Beckwourth trapped beaver in Wyoming. He later lived among the Crow Indians and

married a Crow woman (the Crow thought he was part Native American because of his dark skin). In the early 1850s, Beckwourth settled in California, where he told his life story to Thomas Bonner, a local justice of the peace. In 1856 Bonner published *The Life and Adventures of James P. Beckwourth, Mountaineer, Scout, and Pioneer, and Chief of the Crow Nation of Indians*, supposedly in the mountain man's own words. Some of Beckwourth's old-time pals read it and laughed. Not only had Beckwourth stretched the truth about a few of his adventures, but the Jim they knew had never used fancy, flowery language like this description of his ranch in the Sierra Nevada: "When the weary, toil-worn **emigrant** reaches this valley, he feels himself secure; he can lay himself down and taste refreshing repose, undisturbed by the fear of Indians."

Virginian James P. Beckwourth became a California rancher after several decades of exploring and trapping in the West.

the Great Basin and the Mojave Desert. Other trappers, such as Jim Bridger and Christopher

"Kit" Carson, later became guides for travelers in the West.

Whose Territory?

In the early nineteenth century, the region that now makes up the states of Oregon, Washington, and Idaho and the Canadian province of British Columbia was called the Oregon Country. At first, three nations claimed the area. Spain regarded Oregon as the northern part of its California territory. Great Britain felt that the explorations of Mackenzie and Vancouver gave it a claim to the area. The United States argued that Gray and Lewis and Clark had claimed it for America.

U.S. secretary of state John Quincy Adams settled the matter. In 1818 he made a deal with Britain for joint possession of the Oregon Country. Neither nation owned the region, but people from both nations could enter it. The following year, Adams forged the Adams-Onís Treaty with Spain. Under this **treaty**, Spain dropped its claim to Oregon but got Texas.

William Clark's map of the Lewis and Clark expedition was published in 1814. One of the most influential maps ever made of the American territory, it inspired countless missionaries, traders, and settlers to make the journey west.

The United States got Florida.

By 1825, Adams was president. He tried to divide the Oregon Country with Britain, but at first the two nations could not agree on a border. Then, in 1846, the territory was divided into two parts. The northern part of the Oregon Country joined British Canada. The southern part became the U.S. Oregon Territory. The United States had secured its pathway to the Pacific.

Both Great Britain and the United States claimed the large region known as the Oregon Country, although only a small area of it along the Willamette River had been settled by 1840. In 1846 the two nations agreed on a boundary that gave the northern part of the Oregon Country, along with Vancouver Island, to Britain. Today this area is the Canadian province of British Columbia. The southern or American portion of the Oregon Country was made into territories and, eventually, into the states of Oregon, Washington, and Idaho.

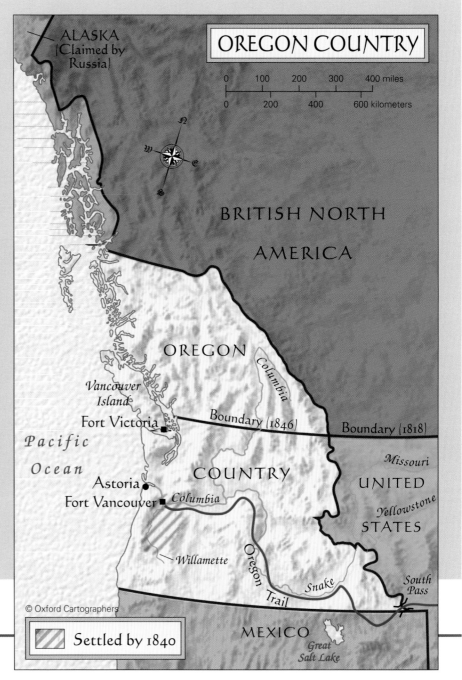

ALASKA (Claimed by Russia)

OREGON COUNTRY

0 100 200 300 400 miles
0 200 400 600 kilometers

BRITISH NORTH AMERICA

OREGON

Columbia

Vancouver Island

Fort Victoria   Boundary (1846)   Boundary (1818)

Pacific Ocean   COUNTRY   Missouri   UNITED

Astoria   Yellowstone
Fort Vancouver   Columbia   STATES

Willamette   Oregon Trail   Snake   South Pass

© Oxford Cartographers

Settled by 1840

MEXICO   Great Salt Lake

MANIFEST DESTINY

 Americans who crossed the Rocky Mountains or went to Texas in the early nineteenth century were entering territory that did not belong to the United States. Many, however, felt that those lands should be part of their country. They saw the Spanish and British claims as a barrier to American settlement and trade. And some felt that because the United States had a new form of democratic government, it had a duty to occupy all of North America.

Thomas Hart Benton, a U.S. senator from Missouri, promoted these ideas. He hated the Adams-Onís Treaty for giving Texas to Spain. In 1827 he wrote these words about the treaty: "The western people have a claim from the laws of God and nature to the exclusive possession of the entire valley of the Mississippi.... Not an inch of its soil should be trod, not a drop of its waters should be drunk, by any foreign power. The American people alone should have it." John Louis O'Sullivan, a New York journalist, shared Benton's views. In 1845 he wrote that the "manifest destiny," or clear fate, of the American people was "to overspread and to possess the whole of the continent." The belief that the United States should acquire more of North America became known as *manifest destiny*. It made Americans feel that taking control of the West was the right thing to do.

Helen Lundeberg's 1934 painting **"Pioneers of the West"** *captures the spirit that had driven Americans westward a century earlier. Under the spell of manifest destiny, Americans saw the West as a land of golden resources and possibilities, and they believed that taming it was their glorious duty.*

Chapter Two

WESTWARD HO!

ven before the United States had a firm claim to Oregon, Americans were drawn to the area. Explorers praised the rich soil, mild weather, and plentiful timber and water of the Columbia River region. More than half a million men, women, and children made the long, hard journey to the distant West during the nineteenth century.

First Settlers

During the 1820s, a few mountain men and Canadian fur traders settled in Oregon, carving out homesteads along the Willamette River, which flows into the Columbia. The British fur-trading post, Fort Vancouver, was located nearby on the bank of the Columbia. Its director, John McLoughlin, helped new set-

Founded in 1825, Fort Vancouver belonged to the British Hudson's Bay trading company (the British government built a military fort there as well). During the early years of settlement in the Pacific Northwest, Fort Vancouver was the hub of the region's economic and social life—and the only place for hundreds of miles that had a piano.

tlers with supplies and advice, whether they came from Canada or the United States.

Americans continued to arrive during the 1830s. A Boston man named Nathaniel Wyeth came to start a business catching and drying fish from Oregon's rivers. Other newcomers were **missionaries** who wanted to spread Christianity among the Native Americans. In 1836 Dr. Marcus Whitman and his wife, Narcissa, founded a mission for the Cayuse Indians near what is now Walla Walla, Washington. Eleven years later, the Whitman mission was the center of a tragic misunderstanding. Smallpox and measles ran wild among the Indians, killing many. Seeing that white people suffered less from the diseases (because they were more used to them), the Cayuse thought that the missionaries were deliberately spreading measles so that whites could take over Indian land. Cayuse warriors attacked the mission, killing the Whitmans and a dozen others. The Indians were wrong about the Whitmans, but they were right about whites wanting their land. Settlers in the Far West would soon push the Native Americans off their homelands and onto **reservations**.

The Oregon Trail

During the late 1830s, a few adventurous Americans followed the tracks of Wyeth and the Whitmans, bringing their goods overland in wagons to start new lives in the Far West.

They were called **emigrants** because they were emigrating, or leaving their own country.

At first, fewer than a hundred people a year went west. But "Oregon fever" spread through the Mississippi Valley and the eastern states as people heard that good land was free for the taking in the Pacific Northwest. The spring of 1843 saw the first large-scale migration. Approximately a thousand people set off from communities along the Missouri River, traveling west in long caravans called wagon trains. The route they followed came to be called the Oregon Trail.

Most emigrants started their journey in Independence, Missouri. From there the trail headed northwest across the Great Plains, which the government had set aside as Indian territory. It passed over prairies covered with tall grasses and wildflowers. Some children felt that the trip was a grand adventure, a picnic that never ended. As the wagons followed the Platte River through Nebraska and into Wyoming, the landscape grew dry and dusty, and strange rock towers and walls jutted from the earth. Eventually, snowcapped peaks appeared on the horizon. The emigrants crossed the Rocky Mountains at South Pass, a broad, low passage that the mountain men had discovered. When the wagon trains crawled down the far side of South Pass, they were halfway to the end of the trail.

West of the pass the trail turned north to

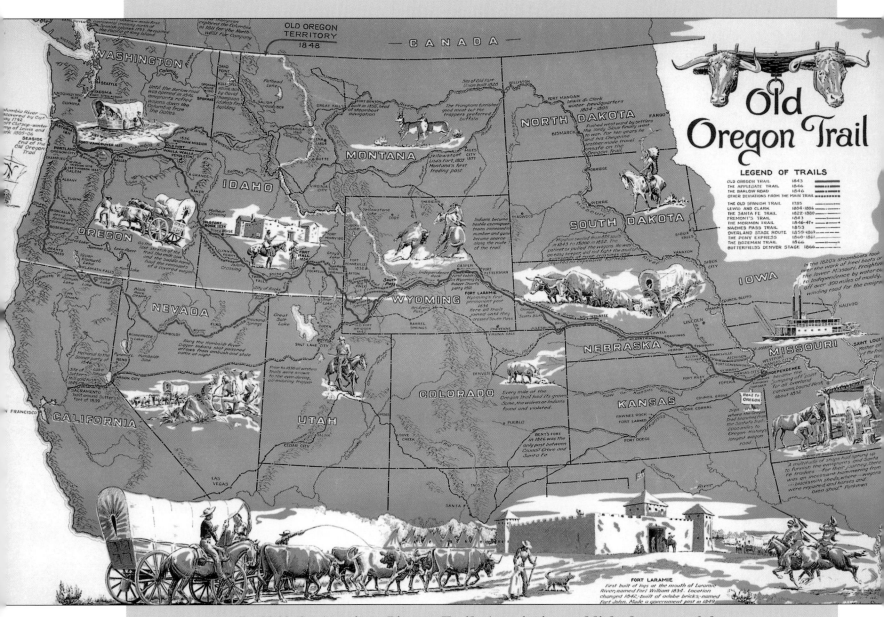

In 1948 the American Pioneer Trails Association published a map of the "Old Oregon Trail" in honor of the one-hundredth anniversary of the creation of the Oregon Territory. The map is filled with colorful bits of Trail lore.

Year after year, wagon trains crossed the plains, mountains, and deserts of the West. More than one emigrant wrote of standing atop a hill and marveling at the sight of a long line of wagons inching across a vast sea of grass. The cloud of dust raised by a wagon train could be seen for many miles and sometimes hung in the air for several days.

meet the Snake River in Idaho. There the trail split. One branch headed southwest across Nevada, then over the Sierra Nevada mountain range to California. Some emigrants went that way, even though California was part of Mexico during the early years of the Trail. The other branch headed northwest along the Snake and then west down the Columbia River. The emigrants used ropes and chains to haul their wagons up some of the steepest slopes along the

SHORTCUTS, DEADLY DELAYS

Travelers on the Oregon Trail wanted to finish the journey as quickly as possible, before supplies ran out, livestock died, and winter rains and snows lashed the wagon trains. They eagerly listened to reports of shortcuts or cutoffs. Sometimes they lost their lives trying to save a few weeks or days.

In 1846, sixty-six-year-old Tabitha Brown traveled the Oregon Trail with her family. When they got to Idaho, her family and several others

As the Donner-Reed party of emigrants crossed the deserts of Nevada, their oxen began to die of exhaustion and starvation. This was just the first of many troubles the group would suffer on its ill-fated shortcut.

left their wagon train to follow a guide who promised to show them a shorter route to the Willamette Valley. The Browns' guide turned out to be a crook who robbed them and left them to suffer Indian attacks and starvation. Some of the travelers died. Tabitha Brown lost her wagon and all of her possessions, but she reached the Willamette Valley alive on Christmas Day—months after the travelers who had not taken the shortcut.

That same year, the Donner-Reed party of emigrants, bound for California, decided to take a shortcut described in a book. Unfortunately, the author had never seen the shortcut. He had only heard about it from some Indians, and his information was poor. The cutoff led the emigrants through Utah's rugged Wasatch Mountains and across the barren Great Salt Desert. Progress was agonizingly slow. The travelers reached the Sierra Nevada late in the season. Snow had closed the mountain passes, and they had to spend the winter miserably in snowbound cabins with little food. Several dozen died, and some of the survivors ate the flesh of the dead. Historians call the Donner-Reed party's fate the worst disaster in wagon train history.

way, then lowered the wagons carefully to keep them from crashing to splinters. Near the end of their journey, they had to choose between a difficult crossing of Oregon's Cascade Mountains or a dangerous raft trip through the falls and rapids of the Columbia. Beyond these barriers lay their goal, the pleasant valley of the Willamette.

Life on the Trail

The average length of an emigrant's journey was 2,200 miles (3,520 kilometers), and many of them walked the whole way! Their canvas-topped wagons were crammed with food, tools, and other vital supplies. Only pregnant women, sick people, and the very old or very young could ride. Others walked alongside the oxen, mules, or horses that pulled their wagons.

Men and boys handled the livestock, rode ahead to scout for water, grass, and good campsites, and hunted deer or buffalo. Fresh meat was a welcome change, because most meals consisted of coffee, beans, bacon, and bread. Women and girls cooked, made and unmade camp, tended young children, and gathered firewood. On the treeless plains they used dried buffalo dung as fuel. They also nursed the sick and injured. Disease and accidents were the main causes of death along the trail.

Fear of Indians haunted many emigrants. One traveler wrote that the people in his wagon train expected "the war whoop and the scalping

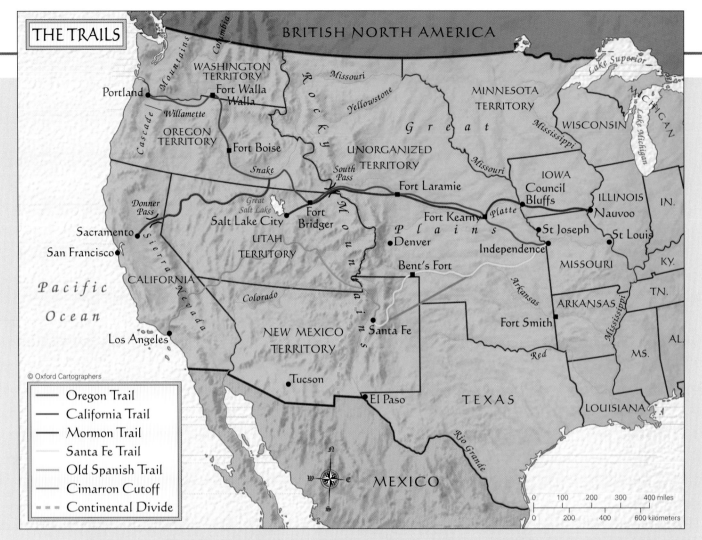

THE TRAILS

BRITISH NORTH AMERICA

Legend:
- Oregon Trail
- California Trail
- Mormon Trail
- Santa Fe Trail
- Old Spanish Trail
- Cimarron Cutoff
- Continental Divide

© Oxford Cartographers

The Oregon Trail is the best-known of the western routes, but there were others.
The California and Mormon trails ran along the Oregon Trail for part of its route, but they
branched off to different destinations after crossing the Rocky Mountains at South Pass. This
pass was the easiest place to cross the Continental Divide, the line along the mountain crests
that marks the division between eastward-flowing waters and those that flow westward.
Farther south, the Santa Fe Trail and the Old Spanish Trail, first traveled by Spanish fortune
hunters and missionaries, linked the Southwest with the towns of the Mississippi valley.

knife" at any moment. But violence was rare. Most emigrants found the Native Americans they met to be friendly, even helpful. Emigrants and Indian women often bartered, trading

"FATHER GOT THE WESTERN FEVER"

 In 1851, thirteen-year-old Martha Gay set off on the Oregon trail with her parents and ten brothers and sisters. They reached Oregon safely and settled in the Willamette Valley. Late in her life, Martha wrote about how her happy childhood in Springfield, Missouri, ended in a journey that no one in the family except her father wanted to make:

We had lived in Springfield three years and were very happy and prosperous and the future looked bright. But father got the Western fever. He had talked about Oregon and the Columbia River for many years and wanted to go there.... Mother was not willing to go. She did not want to undertake the long and dangerous journey with a large family of small children. To cross the plains in those days with ox teams was a fearful undertaking and a tiresome one too. She begged father to give up the notion but he could not.... Mother finally reluctantly consented to go. Father at once set about making arrangements for the journey. He told us of his intention and said he wanted us all to go with him to the new country. He told us about the great Pacific Ocean, the Columbia River, the beautiful Willamette Valley, the great forests and the snowcapped mountains. He then explained the hardships and dangers, the sufferings and the dreary long days we would journey on and on before we would reach Oregon. He then asked if we wanted to go. We rather thought we wanted to stay with our school friends and our societies. But children were expected to do as their parents said in those days and father said we must come. Lovers, sweethearts, and associates were all left behind and we came with our father and mother to Oregon.

Despite warnings of dire fates and the pleas of loved ones who dreaded the journey, thousands of adventurous individuals—mostly men—declared that they were "Going West, By Thunder."

A Mormon frontier settlement in the West. The Mormons' practice of polygamy, a system of marriage that allows men to have multiple wives at the same time, brought them into conflict with U.S. law and custom. Before Utah could become a state, the Mormons officially gave up polygamy.

needles and clothing for fresh fish and vegetables. In return for goods, Indians also helped emigrants find water and cross rivers. Along most of the trail, Native Americans realized that the whites were just passing through, not coming to stay.

The Mormon Migration

In 1830, a man named Joseph Smith founded the Church of Jesus Christ of Latter-Day Saints in New York state. The members of this church, called *Mormons*, found life difficult because many Americans disapproved of their religious beliefs and customs—especially polygamy, a form of marriage that allowed Mormon men to have many wives. The Mormons moved to the Ohio River Valley, but after Smith was killed by an angry mob in Illinois in 1844, their new leader, Brigham Young, decided they should settle in the West, far from other people. In 1846, twelve thousand Mormons traveled to northeastern Utah and settled near the Great Salt Lake. They were just the beginning.

Utah was part of Mexico at the time, but the Mexican government did not care if some Americans settled in this remote region, which was mostly desert. By the late 1860s, more than 50,000 Mormon emigrants had arrived in Utah. The Mormons made the land productive through **irrigation** and hard work, and they hoped that their colony would become an independent country. But not long after the Mormon migration began, conflict between the United States and Mexico would bring an end to Mormon dreams of independence. It would also change the ownership of much of the West.

Chapter Three

TEXAS, THE SOUTHWEST, & CALIFORNIA

Spanish control of Mexico lasted for three hundred years. Over the centuries, Spanish settlers and culture spread northward into Texas, California, and the land between them. The oldest settlement was founded around 1600 at Santa Fe, New Mexico. Starting in the 1760s, Catholic missionaries from Spain and Mexico built missions in California to convert the Indians to Christianity and harness their labor. But Spanish settlers and soldiers were spread thinly over the vast region beyond Mexico's northern border—too thinly to keep Americans out.

Americans in Spanish Territory

Spain wanted the population and economy of its northern borderland to grow, so it offered land to anyone who would bring settlers to Texas. A Missouri man named Moses Austin asked for a land grant, but before he received it, Mexico won independence from Spain in 1821. By the time the new Mexican govern-

The Santa Fe Trail winds through the rugged southwestern landscape. William Becknell, a St. Louis trader who was the first American to travel the route, wrote in his journal: "The next day, after crossing a mountain country, we arrived at Santa Fe and were received with apparent pleasure and joy." His trip launched regular overland trade between St. Louis and Santa Fe.

ment granted the land claim, Moses Austin was dead. His son Stephen Austin took the claim and led three hundred families into Texas, where they settled along the Brazos River. More Americans arrived during the 1820s. In return for land from the Mexican government, they agreed to learn Spanish, become Catholics, and follow Mexican laws.

Americans entered other Spanish regions as well. In 1821, a St. Louis trader named William Becknell took a pack train of mules and merchandise to Santa Fe. He sold his goods for a handsome profit, launching a thriving trade. American merchants followed his route, which became known as the Santa Fe Trail, to swap their cloth and guns for silver, furs, and mules from the Southwest.

Few Americans visited California before Mexico became independent. Most were crewmen on ships that stopped for water and supplies, but some mountain men traveled overland to California. In 1826, Jedediah Smith and several companions crossed the Mojave Desert to Los Angeles. The Spanish ordered them to leave the territory, and one of the trappers later reported that the Native Americans at the Spanish mission were "slaves in every sense of the word."

Mexico was more willing than Spain had been to let Americans trade and settle in California. By the mid-1840s, around seven or eight hundred Americans were living in

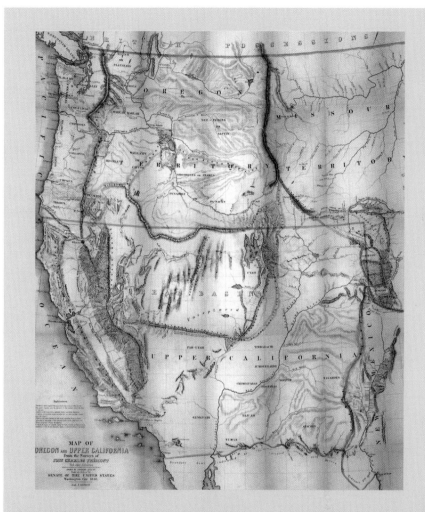

Army officer and explorer John Charles Frémont included this map in an 1845 report on his travels through the Rocky Mountains and beyond. The first map to show all the West, from the Missouri River to the Pacific Ocean, it was widely used and copied during the era of western settlement.

California, mostly along the Sacramento River north of San Francisco. Around that time, a

In late 1835, Mexican troops marched into Texas to stamp out the rebellion that was spreading through the American settlements there. At first the Mexican armies of generals Santa Anna and Urrea were victorious, but in March 1836, during the siege of the Alamo, the Americans proclaimed the independence of the Republic of Texas. Although one phase of the conflict ended when Houston captured Santa Anna at San Jacinto, fighting in the borderlands continued for years.

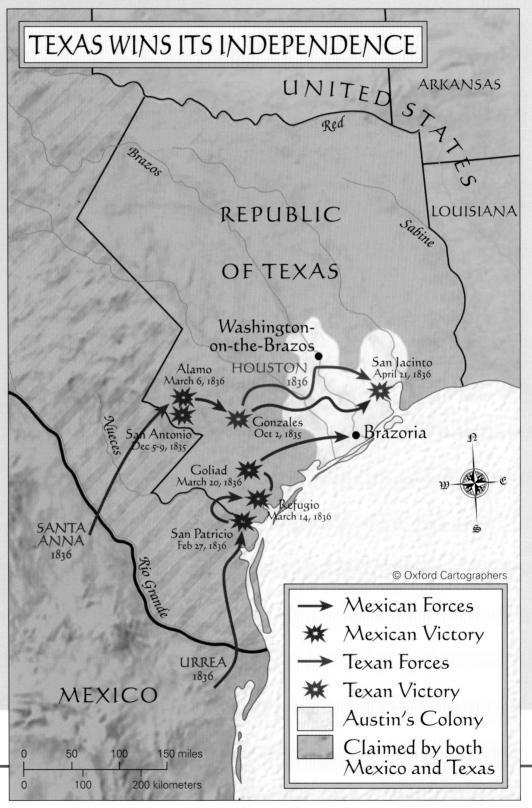

TEXAS WINS ITS INDEPENDENCE

UNITED STATES

ARKANSAS

Red

Brazos

REPUBLIC

LOUISIANA

OF TEXAS

Sabine

Washington-on-the-Brazos

HOUSTON 1836

Alamo
March 6, 1836

San Jacinto
April 21, 1836

Gonzales
Oct 2, 1835

San Antonio
Dec 5-9, 1835

Nueces

Brazoria

Goliad
March 20, 1836

Refugio
March 14, 1836

SANTA
ANNA
1836

San Patricio
Feb 27, 1836

Rio Grande

© Oxford Cartographers

URREA
1836

MEXICO

Mexican Forces
Mexican Victory
Texan Forces
Texan Victory
Austin's Colony
Claimed by both Mexico and Texas

0   50   100   150 miles

0   100   200 kilometers

Land of the Lone Star

Back in Texas, meanwhile, the American settlers were in trouble. Mexico was angry because most of the settlers had failed to keep the earlier agreements they had made and because the United States kept trying to buy Texas. Afraid that Texas was becoming too American, Mexico closed it to American settlers and tried to limit its trade with the United States.

In the mid-1830s, the Americans in Texas decided to fight for independence. Men came from all over the United States to join the fight. General Antonio López de Santa Anna, president of Mexico, sent troops into Texas to crush the revolt. The Americans defeated them in a battle at San Antonio. Santa Anna then overthrew an American-held

U.S. army officer named John C. Frémont explored the West. He felt that California should be part of the United States, and his attractive descriptions of the territory made many Americans agree.

fortress called the Alamo on March 6, 1836. While that fight raged, American Texans declared the independence of the Republic of Texas. Their leader, Sam Houston, attacked Santa Anna at San Jacinto and managed to capture the Mexican president. Humiliated, Santa Anna gave Texas its independence in May 1836. The Texas flag bore a white star on a blue background, earning the new country its nickname: The Lone Star Republic.

Texas wanted to join the United States, but President Andrew Jackson refused. Many Texans were slaveholders, and Jackson did not want to admit another slave state to the nation. The United States was feeling growing tension over the issue of slavery. A new slave state would have upset the important balance in government between senators from slave states and those from free states. By the mid-1840s, however, the idea of manifest destiny had grown stronger. Congress and President James Polk were ready to **annex** Texas. The Lone Star Republic became the twenty-eighth state in 1845.

War with Mexico

Tension between the United States and Mexico remained high. The two nations disagreed over borders, and Mexico claimed that the U.S. annexation of Texas was illegal. Yet the annexation wasn't enough to satisfy Americans who wanted their nation to grow. President Polk also tried to buy New Mexico and California.

Sam Houston commanded volunteer soldiers at the Battle of San Jacinto in eastern Texas. With 783 men, he killed 630 Mexicans and captured another 730.

TRAGEDY AT GOLIAD

 The saying goes, "Remember the Alamo," but do you remember Goliad? After the fall of the Alamo, some Texans under the command of Colonel James Fannin were retreating from a fort at Goliad when Mexican general José de Urrea surrounded them. The Texans surrendered, and Urrea turned them over to an officer named Nicolás de la Portilla. Urrea ordered Portilla to treat the prisoners fairly, but then Santa Anna ordered him to kill them. Portilla spent a night torn by uncertainty before deciding to obey Santa Anna. He ordered the more than three hundred Texans shot. Americans in Texas and the rest of the country were furious. When word of the massacre spread, Sam Houston received enough volunteers and ammunition to attack and defeat Santa Anna.

Mexican president and general Antonio López de Santa Anna was among the prisoners captured at San Jacinto. Many Texans wanted to hang him, but Houston released him after he signed a treaty giving Texas its independence. When Santa Anna returned to Mexico, however, he was thrown out of office, and the Mexican government rejected the treaty.

When Mexico refused, he sent U.S. troops into a border region claimed by both Mexico and the United States. As he had expected, the Mexicans tried to drive them out. Polk declared war in May 1846, saying that Mexico had "shed American blood on American soil."

Some Americans, including future president Abraham Lincoln, viewed the war as an unjust land grab. They believed that Polk had deliberately started a war with Mexico in the hope that the United States would win by force the territory that Mexico had refused to sell. They also feared that slavery would expand into any new territory taken from Mexico. Others welcomed

Once President Polk had declared war on Mexico, in May 1846, he unveiled a three-part plan of attack. One part was to seize and hold disputed territory on the Texas-Mexico border. A second part was to take control of New Mexico and California (this effort was aided by the Bear Flag Revolt in June 1846, in which Americans in California rebelled against Mexican rule). The third part was to capture Mexico City, in the heart of the enemy's country. Despite heroic resistance by the defenders of the Mexican capital, U.S. forces had achieved all three goals by September 1847. The victorious United States forced Mexico to give up about half of its territory in the Treaty of Guadalupe Hidalgo.

the chance to extend America's boundaries. Even before learning of the war, a handful of Americans in northern California had declared California an independent state called the Bear Flag Republic. Army officer John Charles Frémont and mountain man Kit Carson joined the Bear Flag rebels. Soon a U.S. Navy ship seized several Mexican ports and annexed California in the name of the United States. Many *californios,* or Mexicans living in

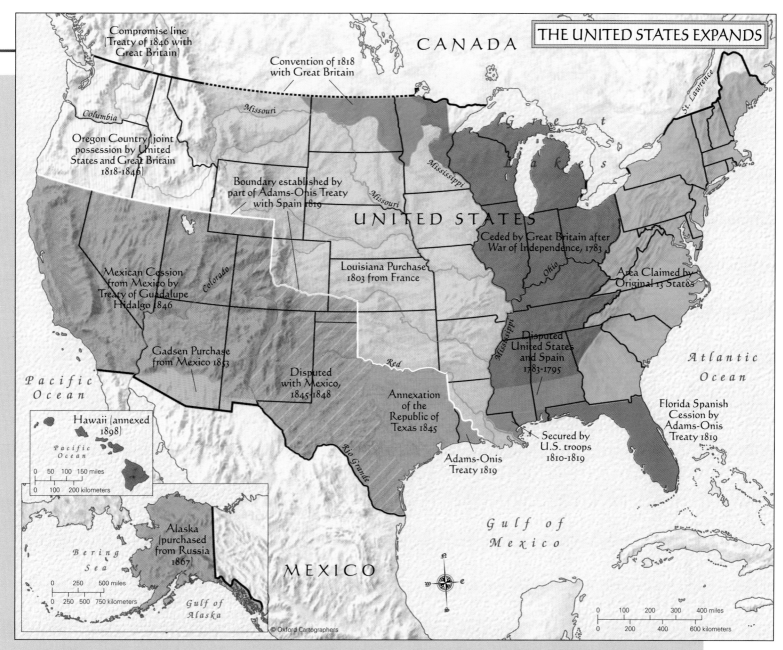

CANADA

Compromise line
(Treaty of 1846 with
Great Britain)

Convention of 1818
with Great Britain

Columbia

Missouri

Oregon Country (joint
possession by United
States and Great Britain
1818-1846)

Boundary established by
part of Adams-Onis Treaty
with Spain 1819

Missouri

Mississippi

UNITED STATES

Great Lakes

St. Lawrence

Ceded by Great Britain after
War of Independence, 1783

Ohio

Area Claimed by
Original 13 States

Mexican Cession
from Mexico by
Treaty of Guadalupe
Hidalgo 1846

Colorado

Louisiana Purchase
1803 from France

Gadsen Purchase
from Mexico 1853

Disputed
with Mexico,
1845-1848

Red

Disputed
United States
and Spain
1783-1795

Mississippi

Atlantic
Ocean

Pacific
Ocean

Annexation
of the
Republic of
Texas 1845

Secured by
U.S. troops
1810-1819

Florida Spanish
Cession by
Adams-Onis
Treaty 1819

Hawaii (annexed
1898)

Pacific
Ocean

0 50 100 150 miles

0   100   200 kilometers

Rio Grande

Adams-Onis
Treaty 1819

Alaska
(purchased
from Russia
1867)

Bering
Sea

Gulf of
Alaska

MEXICO

Gulf of
Mexico

0   250   500 miles

0 250 500 750 kilometers

© Oxford Cartographers

0   100   200   300   400 miles

0   200   400   600 kilometers

In 1783, after the Revolutionary War, the United States emerged as a nation. By that time, it already stretched west far beyond the original thirteen British colonies. The United States continued to expand westward, acquiring territory from France, Spain, Great Britain, and Mexico, and simply seized the lands of many Native American nations. By the 1850s the dream of manifest destiny had come true, and the United States stretched from the Atlantic Ocean to the Pacific.

Texas, the Southwest, & California

John Tallis's map of Mexico, California, and Texas was published as part of an atlas in 1851, just a few years after the United Stated had won its new western borders. Many maps and atlases of that period featured illustrations, such as Tallis's picture "Gold Washing," which shows the California Gold Rush of 1849.

California, resisted this takeover. By January 1847, though, California was in U.S. hands.

The Mexican War ended later that year when U.S. commander Winfield Scott captured Mexico City. In 1848 Mexico signed the Treaty of Guadalupe Hidalgo, giving California, Nevada, Utah, and parts of Arizona, New Mexico, Colorado, and Wyoming to the United States. Five years later, in a land deal called the Gadsden Purchase, the United States bought more territory in southern Arizona and southern New Mexico. A river called the Río

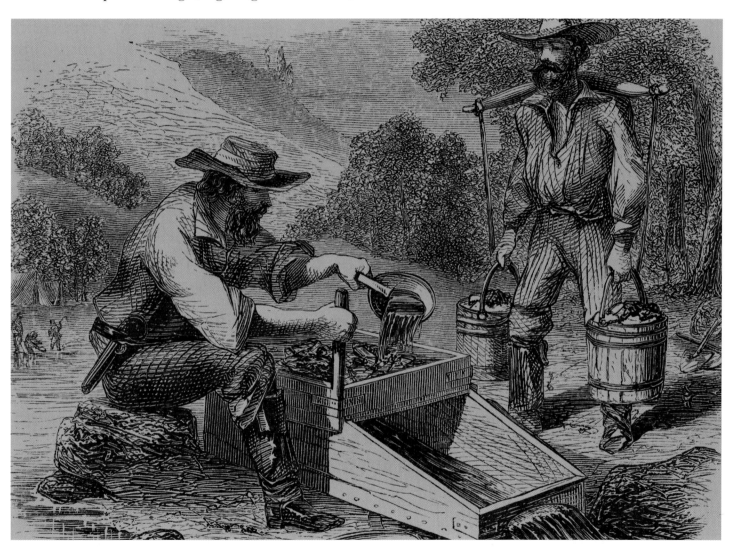

California gold prospectors sift bucketloads of stream bottom, hoping that heavy flecks of gold will remain after the sand and muck are washed away.

Another illustrated map from 1851 shows all of North America. Some of the pictures represent sights that had become symbols of America, such as Niagara Falls and the wapiti deer (an elk). In the upper left are Cossacks—Russian soldiers—meant to illustrate the fact that Russia controlled Alaska at that time.

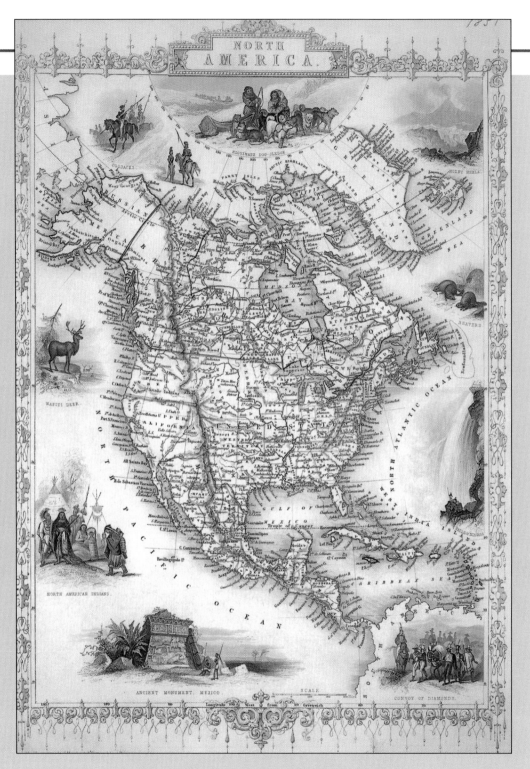

Grande became the border between Mexico and the United States, and it remains the border today.

The California Gold Rush

A few weeks before the Treaty of Guadalupe Hidalgo was signed, John Marshall, an American in northern California, made a discovery that greatly increased the value of the new U.S. territory. Bending down to pick a shining pebble from a stream, he realized it was gold. When word got out, people hurried to the area by the thousands, hoping to pluck fortunes from the streams that ran down from the Sierra Nevada. The California Gold Rush had begun.

Most of the 100,000 or so hopeful prospectors who poured into California by land and sea were called *Forty-Niners* because they arrived in 1849. About half were Americans. Mexicans, Australians, Europeans, South

Americans, and Chinese also joined the rush. Boomtowns of shacks and tents dotted the high canyons of the Sierra Nevada. Gambling halls, saloons, and stores sprang up to serve the needs of the miners—and the merchants who ran them made the biggest fortunes of all. Very few of the miners ever found enough gold to make them rich. But when gold fever died down, many miners stayed on in California to become farmers, businesspeople, or laborers. The territory's population grew so fast that California became a state in 1850, just four years after the Bear Flag Revolt. Oregon became a state nine years later.

The United States now stretched from the Atlantic to the Pacific and from Canada to Mexico. The Indians had been the first to inhabit Texas and the Pacific Coast, and Spain and Great Britain were the first to explore them. But in the end, the Americans won the West.

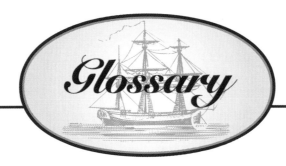

Glossary

annex: to enlarge a nation or state by adding territory that was formerly outside its borders

emigrant: one who leaves his or her native country to settle somewhere else

irrigation: use of canals, wells, and other manmade features to bring water to dry land so that it can be farmed

migration: mass movement of people from one place to another

missionary: one who works to convert others to his or her religion

reservation: area assigned to Native Americans by the U.S. government

treaty: formal agreement between nations

ABOUT THE AUTHOR

Rebecca Stefoff is the author of many nonfiction books for children and young adults. Her books on American history include the other volumes in Marshall Cavendish's North American Historical Atlases series, as well as *Women Pioneers* (1995), *Children of the Westward Trail* (1996), *The Oregon Trail in American History* (1997), and *The Opening of the American West*. Stefoff lives in Portland, Oregon, the site of several major research centers for people interested in the history of the West and the Oregon Trail.

Map List

ABOUT THE HISTORICAL MAPS

The historical maps used in this book are primary source documents found in The Library of Congress Map Division. You will find these maps on pages: 15, 22, 33, 40, 42.

Chronology

1787 First American ship reaches the Oregon coast.

1803-1806 Meriwether Lewis and William Clark lead a U.S. expedition to Oregon and back.

1819 Adams-Onís Treaty ends U.S. claim to Texas and sets border between Spanish California and Oregon Country. United States and Great Britain agree to share Oregon.

1821 Moses Austin of Missouri receives land in Texas. Mexico (including Texas) wins independence from Spain. First American traders reach New Mexico.

1830s American missionaries and settlers arrive in Oregon Country.

1836 American settlers declare Texas an independent republic. Mexican troops win the Battle of the Alamo.

1840s Americans begin settling in California, which belongs to Mexico.

1843 First large-scale westward migration of settlers on the Oregon Trail.

1845 Texas becomes a state.

1846 United States declares war on Mexico. Americans in California form an independent state called the Bear Flag Republic. Mormons begin settling in Utah. United States and Great Britain divide the Oregon Country.

1848 Treaty of Guadalupe Hidalgo ends Mexican War and gives California, Utah, and Nevada, and parts of New Mexico, Arizona and Colorado, and Wyoming to the United States. Gold is discovered in California.

1850 California becomes a state.

1853 In the Gadsden Purchase, the United States acquires additional land in southern New Mexico and southern Arizona.

1859 Oregon becomes a state.

Further Reading

Alter, Judith. *Growing Up in the Old West.* New York: Franklin Watts, 1989.

Altman, Linda Jacobs. *The California Gold Rush in American History.* Springfield, NJ: Enslow, 1997.

Bial, Raymond. *Frontier Home.* Boston: Houghton Mifflin, 1993.

Blumberg, Rhoda. *The Great American Gold Rush.* New York: Bradbury Press, 1989.

Butrille, Susan G. *Women's Voices from the Oregon Trail.* Boise, ID: Tamarack Books, 1993.

Cavan, Seamus. *Lewis and Clark and the Route to the Pacific.* New York: Chelsea House, 1991.

Duncan, Dayton. *People of the West.* Boston: Little, Brown, 1996.

Freedman, Russell. *Children of the Wild West.* New York: Clarion Books, 1983.

Press, Petra. *A Multicultural Portrait of the Move West.* New York: Marshall Cavendish, 1994.

Schanzer, Rosalyn, editor. *Gold Fever! Tales from the California Gold Rush.* Washington, D.C.: National Geographic Society, 1999.

Schlissel, Lillian. *The Way West: Journal of a Pioneer Woman.* New York: Simon & Schuster Books for Young Readers, 1993.

Stefoff, Rebecca. *Children of the Westward Trail.* Brookfield, CT: Millbrook Press, 1996.

——————. *The Oregon Trail in American History.* Springfield, NJ: Enslow, 1997.

——————. *Women Pioneers.* New York: Facts On File, 1995.

Stein, R. Conrad. *The Story of the Lone Star Republic.* Chicago: Children's Press, 1988.

Wexler, Sanford. *Westward Expansion: An Eyewitness History.* New York: Facts On File, 1991.

WEBSITES

New Perspectives on the West, based on the eight-part public television series *The West.*
www.pbs.org/weta/thewest

Information on westward expansion and Native Americans; links to dozens of other pages.
www.americanwest.com

In Search of the Oregon Trail, based on the public television series *The Oregon Trail.*
www.pbs.org/opb/oregontrail

Handbook of Texas Online, with information about history and links to other sites.
www.tsha.utexas.edu/handbook/online

California Historical Society, with links to other sites.
www.calhist.org

Utah History Encyclopedia
www.media.utah.edu/UHE

Index